Everything You Need to Know About ...

Writing Poetry

Simplified

Helen Iles

First published 2005 Paperback edition.

Second Release 2017 Paperback edition.

Third Release 2019 Paperback edition

Copyright © 2005 Helen Iles.

ISBN-13: 978-1-922343-04-8

Linellen Press
265 Boomerang Road
Oldbury, Western Australia 6121

www.linellenpress.com.au

Dedication

This book is dedicated to all my students who always wanted more, and to Lissie.

May you continue to write your poetry.

Contents

Introduction

The idea for this book came from the vast range of research notes compiled while developing class lessons on poetry styles and poetic forms. Those notes form the basis of this book.

During many years teaching creative writing, I have met numerous writers who can churn out fantastic stories full of drama and intrigue, produce page after page of delightful descriptive prose, craft superb and logical articles that grace the pages of glossy magazines yet reel in horror when asked to produce a few simple lines of poetry.

Why is it some writers panic when asked to write something succinct and clear using as few words as possible? The craft of storytelling requires the ability to structure a story in a logical sequence, develop realistic characters, make locations come alive and hone it all to the bone so it is produced in the least amount of words possible. This in a nutshell is the craft of storytelling.

Writing poetry requires the ability to structure a point in a logical form or sequence, describe scenes and images with such emotion that it stirs the reader's emotions, using as few words as possible. This, very loosely, is very much the craft of writing poetry. Not much different to storytelling, is it?

Poetry can be as complicated, or as simple, as the writer wants to make it.

Written in simple terms for the layman, this book provides a wide range of poetry styles and forms so the new poet can spread their wings and take the pen-ultimate challenge of becoming a modern day poet.

The styles are listed in alphabetical order and contain an example poem for reference. The examples are not intended to be works of art but are a simple attempt by a lay poet to master, or at least complete, the style challenge.

A glossary of general poetry terms is provided so the new poet can identify some of the skills used in forming, shaping or producing mood, pace and emphasis within a poem.

❧

What is Poetry?

Definition: Poetry is a vehicle where heightened expression is delivered in lines rather than sentences, with emphasis placed on sound, rhythm and meaning to produce an image that creates a heightened emotional response in the reader.

In simpler terms, it is a form of communication between two people, the person composing the poem and the person for whom it is intended, whether that be the reader or the person to whom the poem is recited.

True poetry is not like ordinary speech in any way. It is the careful crafting of words and rhythms to paint a picture and express the poet's emotions in such a way the reader's emotions are touched by the words selected.

Poetry comes from a Greek word 'to make', because poems are indeed made or constructed. They are produced by the careful selection of thoughts and words, are shaped to form an image, one thought flowing to another, linking the image wherever possible so that the poet's feelings are felt and seen by the reader. The true poet has an uncanny gift for selecting words that say so much, yet say it so economically. It is through that careful word selection that the poet best plies his trade.

Note:

Poetry should be written firstly for the pleasure of the poet, and secondly for the enjoyment of others. So read your poems aloud. It is the best method of telling if a poem flows or jars in any way, and is the best way for an audience to appreciate it in the context it was meant. It is then important to edit what does not sound fluent or effective.

Once a writer understands the concept of form or poetic style, the reading of a poem can take on new meaning. By analysing why those particular words were used and why they were arranged in that particular sequence or line length can change the whole view of the piece and its meaning. This is where the selection of poetic form can be important. Always read poetry with a view to feeling the poet's emotions, with a view to seeing the picture they paint so you can feel the whole experience to its fullest extent. This is why poetic forms exist.

Today, right now, we will start the layman's journey to becoming a poet. It is important to note however that, while attempting to follow a particular poetry style, if a poem takes a life and form of its own on its way to completion you must let it follow its own path. Staying religiously to the form for the sake of mastering the style may well destroy an otherwise perfect poem.

Enjoy the journey.

General Poetry Terms

The following terminologies should be noted and practiced by new and established poets. A basic understanding of their meaning and purpose will allow poets to experiment and use these techniques to improve the structure or sound of their poems.

Alliteration	Alliteration is the repeated use of a consonant sound to produce a desired effect. For example, **flickering flames fired** produces the image of a crackling open fire.
Assonance	Assonance is a likeness of sounds rather than rhyme itself. The vowels sound the same but the consonants are different. Example: came and gain. It also sometimes called *'near rhyme'*.
Caesura	A caesura is a break or pause in a line of poetry which produces a marked change in the tone, argument or flow of sound. It should be used sparingly to produce the greatest impact.

For example:

Guilt wracked and ridden he sinks

Falls into the bottle and screams.   Aloud.

Consonance	Consonance is the repetition of the same stressed end consonants with different vowel sounds. Example: quick, lark; soap, leap. When used at the end of the line it is also called *'near rhyme'*.
Couplets	Couplets consist of two lines that work together, usually of the same length and rhythm and generally rhyming. They can stand alone (closed couplet) or be part of a longer poem.

The Heroic Couplet is two lines written in iambic pentameter. (See meter)

An Alexandrine Couplet is two lines of iambic hexameter that rhyme. (See meter) |
| End Rhyme | The word at the end of one line rhymes with the terminating word of another line. |
| End Stopped | A line that is end stopped has ceased at a natural pause or logical completion so that a comma, semicolon or full stop is appropriate, if punctuation is used.

An end stopped line is the opposite of an enjambed line. |

Enjambment	Opposite to end stopped, an enjambed line is where the thought, phrase or rhythm runs on from one line to the next. The technique should be used sparingly for best effect.
Feminine Rhyme	Rhymes that end with the stress or accent placed on the second last syllable - usually end with 'ing' (e.g. wishing, hoping, dreaming) but not always.
Internal Rhyme	Internal rhyme can occur in two ways. Firstly the words that rhyme can be contained within the line rather than at its end. Secondly a word in the middle of the line can rhyme with the word at the end of the same line. For example:

In the Autumn <u>dark</u> he sits

contemplating the <u>stark</u> reality of life

from a park bench

beneath the <u>trees</u> he <u>sees</u>

his life now nearly done

his family mostly gone

and he remembers long

Meter	Meter is the rhythm built within a poem and is determined by the length of lines written. Meter is generally referred to in syllables or feet.

The various meters are as follows:

Meter	Feet	Syllables
Monometer	one	2
Dimeter	two	4
Trimeter	three	6
Tetrameter	four	8
Pentameter	five	1 0
Hexameter	six	1 2
Heptameter	seven	1 4
Octameter	eight	1 6

Combine these with the various stress rhythms such as anapest and iamb to produce mood and pace.

Onomatopoeia

Onomatopoeia is when the word used imitates the sound it makes e.g. clackety-clack, snap, whistle, hiss. The use of onomatopoeia produces strong images in the reader's mind.

Poetic licence

Poetic licence is said to be used when a poet bends the rules. Assonance in a way is using poetic licence. It is important that the poet knows the rules before they break the rules.

Portmanteau	This is a word form, an artificial word made up of parts of other words. It is used to best effect in Jabberwocky or Nonsense Poems and will be useful to know when attempting the Jabberwocky style.
	Portmanteau words have two meanings because they are two words made into one. For example: combining 'angry' and 'short' makes *angorty*; 'trundling' and 'tromping' makes *trompling*; 'friendly' and 'strife' makes *frife*. For best effect, it is important to make sure the word created is not an actual word.
Qasida	Pronounced kasida. This Arabic form of poetry, while mentioned, is not covered in this book. The many rules of this relatively long poem, in my opinion, takes it beyond the realms of fun poetry for lay poets.
Rhyme	Rhyme exists where the vowel and/or consonants of two or more words sound the same or similar.
	Monosyllabic rhyme is masculine e.g. old, bold, gold.
	Polysyllabic rhyme is feminine e.g. ending, blend-ing, because the end syllable is softer (unstressed).

Rhyming Schemes	Stanzas, or the shape of stanzas, are usually shaped by rhymes. Rhyming schemes are defined by the rhyme of the first line and where it comes next in the poem. Usually the first rhyme sequence is titled 'a'. The next rhyme sound is 'b' and next rhyme sound is 'c', and so on.
	It is important to adhere to the rhyming schemes indicated in the poetic forms that follow to remain true to form.
Rhythm	Rhythm is created by placing emphasis or stress on syllables within the poem. Some syllables are stressed and some are not. This is commonly called the metre of the poem.
	The rhythm of a line or poem encourages the thought and feelings of the poem to be felt.
	There are four main types of stress patterns used in poetry. These should become familiar terms to the poet.
	They are as follows:

Anapestic or anapest.

The stress is on the third syllable, after two preceding unstressed syllables.

Dactylic or dactyl

The first syllable is stressed followed by

two unstressed syllables.

Iambic or Iamb

The first syllable is unstressed, the second syllable is stressed.

Trochaic or trochee

The first syllable is stressed, the second syllable unstressed.

Simile

A simile compares one image to another, saying one image is 'like' another. It differs from the metaphor, which says one image *is* another. Metaphors and similes are powerful tools when writing poetry.

Stanzas

A stanza is the manner in which a poem is laid out, in effect its shape. Stanzas can consist of quatrains, heroic couplets, tercets, a combination of any of the above, or any other layout required to achieve the purpose and meaning of the poem.

Tercet

A tercet is a poem of three lines. The three lines can be part of a longer poem, or they may stand alone. The lines can have rhythm or no rhythm, have rhyme or no rhyme.

Example

Frog on a lily pad, its eyes all agog

For it had spied its dinner

Black gecko on a log.

Poetry Styles

There are many forms and styles of poetry that the new poet can experiment with. The following pages have brought together styles from around the world, styles which are not only fun and challenging to write, but allows the poet to unchain their creativity while mastering the rules.

These are only a sampling of the many poetic forms in existence, given that poetry has been around since the dark and middle ages. I have selected the styles on their suitability for lay poets to begin their first steps towards laureateship.

It is important to note that the whole aim of poetry is to produce memorable images while being economical with words, and to have the reader hold that image in their mind for a long time - even better if the reader commits it to memory for later recital.

The best poems are created by poets who feel passionate, almost obsessive, about their subject or who are present when a mood or atmosphere so affects them that they have to write it down. It is therefore wise to travel the distance, go to places glorious and awe inspiring, experience life and emotions, rather than play with the styles while sitting at the kitchen table.

Unlock, Create, Enjoy!

Poetry Styles

A

Abecedarian Poem

An abecedarian poem is one where each line or verse commences with consecutive letters of the alphabet.

This is a fun and creative way to start writing poetry. The poem can be written in rhyming style or non-rhyming.

Naturally the object of the exercise is to produce an image or story, as in the example below.

The A-Z of Life

Annie was a Mountain Bear
Buelis was a goat
Carlos was a Mexican boy
Deidre was a dope
Each of them lived on the hill
foraging in their way
gathering up the food they'd need to
hibernate winter away.
Idiots don't plan ahead,
just frolic in good times
kicking up their silly heels,
laughingly telling rhymes.
'Mustn't work too hard,' she warned,
'Nothing's worth the toil.'
Obviously those words would be
poor Deidre's downfall.

Quick did come the winter with
raging thunderstorms
Snow did fall down metres thick
Treacherously it swarmed,
Underneath the blizzards frost
very warm at best
were the three wise gatherers
xenial in their nest.
Yet outside in the blustery night that blew so
bitterly
ZZZZedded off poor Deidre ... permanently

Acrostic Poem

An Acrostic poem is one in which the first letters (usually) form a word or message relating to the subject. This style of poetry dates back as far as the 4th century, and is another fun and creative way to start writing poetry.

A Double Acrostic poem has the first letters and the last letters in each line stating a message.

Example: Single Acrostic

White Swan

White and majestic
Her neck arches gracefully
In silent motion
Turning yet seemingly unmoving,
Ever the lake's ballerina.

Superb, she drifts on tiptoe
Watches the lake
And glides to its centre
Nonchalant, and always queen of her domain.

B

Ballads

A ballad is a narrative poem (or song) that tells a story. It is written in short stanzas of two or four lines and often has a refrain (or repeated line). The ballad stanza generally rhymes the second and fourth lines. The rhythm of the lines is very important as it provides tension and release to the poem. Most ballads consist of alternating lines of 8 syllables (or 4 feet), and six syllables (or 3 feet). They are usually in iambic rhythm, that is, the stress or accent is on every second syllable.

Traditionally ballads were meant to be sung, and therefore are narrated impersonally and deal with folk legends or events that are told simplistically. They can also express love or hate, fear or wonder at the physical or supernatural worlds. It is the story within the lines that sustains the reader's interest.

Example:

And the Tree Bleeds

In a deep part of the forest
in the hours of the dark
a huntsman finds his target
yet his aim is off its mark.
And a tree bleeds.

Mid the throes of confrontation
'tween the chippies and the greens,
a spike is driven deeply
for the cutter's hand to glean.
And the tree bleeds.

Yet across expansive forests
the conservationists hard strive
to fight the senseless slaughter
and keep the earth alive.
And the trees sigh.

Yet greed soon reaps its plunder
and strips the trembling land
bares its soul unto the sky
reducing it to sand.
And the trees die.

Across this wide vast nation
where despotism is rife
they kill our land and future
wipe out essential life.
And the trees cry.

Until man heeds the warning
that killing trees is bad
I watch the devastation
and feel immensely sad.
And still the trees bleed.

In a deep part of the forest
where a bullet missed its mark
a pool of red upon the ground
deepens the earth
in dark resinated blood.

Traditional Bush Verse

This style usually has a rhyming pattern of some form or another. Some are written in quatrains, while others contain longer stanzas.

The subject matter usually pertains to:-

a) the elements of the bush, such as cattle dogs, stock horses, stockmen or drovers,

b) elements of weather that affect the bush, or

c) the personalities who live there,

d) heroic feats,

e) places or trails travelled,

f) flora and fauna, or

g) political send-ups of the day.

Generally, when portraying a country's outback, strongly recognisable elements should be seen within the poem.

Poems can be serious or humorous.

Rhyming schemes for traditional Bush verse are many and varied. Examples are:

- 6 line stanzas rhyming   abcbdb
- 6 line stanzas rhyming   abbacc
- Quatrains rhyming   abab
- Quatrains rhyming   aabb
- 8 line stanzas rhyming   ababcdcd

Example: aabb rhyming scheme

Billabong Spirit

White teethed children, black faces gleam
Frolic in water 'neath Coolibah stream
Watched by old women and young bucks fishing
When they noticed a small piccaninny was missing

'Where is Imgali?' the old ladies cried
Rods dropped to the banks as the young bucks tried
To find young Imgali, the youngest tribe daughter,
Three searched the bushes, two dived into water.

'She been playing by wet logs,' one child called out
'I see'd her in water there splashin' about.
She be laughin' and squealin' just moments ago
But where she gone now . oh hell … I dunno.'

Young bucks dropped to coolness, line breasted the water
Soon pulled up the body of tribe's youngest daughter
'Imgali! Imagali!' the old ladies screamed.
The kids all forbid now to swim in the stream.

And the young bucks no longer can dangle their line
Lest they bring up her spirit with Barra entwined
Yet they sit on the rocks there and solemnly wish
As they watch her swim naked - Imagli, the fish.

❧

Bush Verse can also be free verse (that is, having an internal rhyme without a static rhyming scheme), and still emote the imagery of the great outback.

The Eagle

I saw the eagle
deep brown majesty
soar aloft,
above the plains,
above yonder towering tree tops,
his wings borne wide,
and white tipped.
Wind ship.

Grandiose Lord of the skies
he flies
effortlessly,
master of that endless space,
a spirit to indigenous race
who hold him as a sign
of courage and strength,

Yet we of cult;
of no tribal lore;
stand only in awe
of his grace;
of his kingdom and place
not realising that he holds the cosmic key
to being truly free.

Perfection,
in reflection, he is
master of the wing,
of the wind,
of the land;
he has the admiration of man.

As I watch him
his wings in gentle windswept song,
strokes sky,
shadows land,
so grand;
so proud ..

I can see the eagle clearer now
Feel the eagle.
at one with himself.
Maybe too, if I try
I could be that eagle.

Blank Verse

Blank verse is written in iambic tetrameter, pentameter or hexameter, that is the stress or accent is on every second syllable, and each line consists of either eight, ten or twelve distinct beats. If you start with eight beats in the first line, every line has eight beats. The lines are unrhymed, thus giving the form the name blank verse.

This form is commonly used for telling a story or thinking about ideas and feelings, and is a great way to start writing poetry because you are not hampered by trying to end with a rhyme. You are also not compelled to end a statement by the end of a line, but can roll the line over to the next (called enjambment), provided you maintain the set beats chosen in the flow of your speech.

There is no set limit to the amount of lines written in blank verse, the divisions being called verse paragraphs.

Example:

Life Wind Blows

The wind blows nonchalant upon my life
Flaps handkerchiefs that yesterday mopped tears
Tears that fall today and tissues dissolve
Stockings stroll, zephyr pushed round corridors
Authorative steps on a carpet green
As doors that once were open wide slam shut.

Clouds creep over the sun, darkening day
As the shirt of femininity flips
As the skirt of elegance flutters
Knickers that I bought to impress you swing
The lacy frills where your cupped hand rested
Starts a fresh flow as rain begins to fall.

I shall leave my mistakes strung on the line
Let nature wash away the stains of life
If memories still flow when evening's done
I'll trash this power suit, start life anew
And be wiser for the experience.

C

Choka

Choka is a form of Japanese poetry that consists of alternating lines of five and seven syllables. The length of the poem is not fixed, but the ending is signified by an extra line of seven syllables.

Example:

> Fire blazes brightly
> Reflects on your perfect face
> Flickers in your eyes
> Reveals your sensuous thoughts
> Beneath a jewelled sky
> Passion flows back over flame
> Heating skin like fire
> Wine sipped as thoughts acknowledge
> I smile and reach for your hand.

Cinquain

Cinquains come in two forms, the traditional and the modern. They can be fun to write and are easily mastered.

The traditional cinquain contains a set number of syllables per line and can be written on any subject.

a)   Line 1   is two syllables

b)   Line 2   is four syllables

c)   Line 3   is six syllables

d)   Line 4   is eight syllables

e)   Line 5   is two syllables

Example:

Subway
Underground rail
that rips through tunnel dark
taking me swift to journey's end
Eyes closed.

The **modern cinquain** is a short form of poetry that consists of the following:

a)   Line 1 is one word, a noun

b)   Line 2 two adjectives describing the noun

c)   Line 3 three verbs (usually 'ing' verbs) that describe actions performed by the noun

d)   Line 4 a complete four word statement expressing a feeling about the noun

e)   Line 5 another noun of one word that means the same as the first noun or relates strongly to it.

Cinquains have no title - usually the first line indicates the poem subject.

Example:

Sustenance
Crunchy; tasty
Relieving; satisfying; filling;
Silence my stomach stuff
Food!

Cinquain Suite

A cinquain suite is a series of cinquain poems relating to the same subject and can be written in either form. Cinquain Suites are given titles.

Example:

Sam

Sam
black velvet; white toothed;
shoe chewing; hole digging; house re-arranging
New child of mine
Rotweiler

Rotweiler
white fanged; slobby mouthed;
domineering; horse-chasing; house-wrecking;
Bane of my life
Sam!!

Sam
full grown; idiot faced;
fully-obedient; night-prowling; house-guarding
Protector of my life
Friend.

෨

Clarity Pyramid

This relatively new form of poetry is based on syllable count and makes a point through its layout to clarify points or details about the first line, the title. Its requirement to increase syllables throughout the lines and centering each line on the page produces a triangular or pyramid shape.

The poem is broken into two triplets (sets of three lines) and a single line to finish.

Line 1 contains one syllable, is in bold print and capitalized, and becomes the title.

Line 2 contains two syllables which clarifies the first line or is a synonym of the first line.

Line 3 contains three syllables and further clarifies the title.

Line 4 is blank.

Line 5 contains five syllables that expresses the poet's view about line 1.

Line 6 contains six syllables and again expresses the view of the title

Line 7 contains seven syllables and continues the viewpoint of Lines 5 and 6.

Lines 5, 6, and 7 combined should produce an image or life event expressed by the poet.

Line 8 contains eight syllables. It is contained within quotation marks and is a statement that defines the title word.

Example

Rose
Flower
Heady bloom

Majestic glory
Standing like a princess
Waiting to be plucked from grace

"a garden's true magnificence"

୬

Clerihew

A form of humorous verse, the Clerihew is a four line jingle that makes a statement, or epitomises a notable character in a light or whimsical way.

The quatrain is rhymed as two couplets aa bb. Lines are of unequal length, more resembling prose than poetry. The subject's name usually ends the first line - occasionally the second.

Example:

Freud

> A remarkable man was Seigmund Freud
> For deep into people's minds he toyed
> Categorised mental states I'm told
> And forever now we're pigeon-holed!

Charming

> Who can forget that charming Rhett Butler
> Who with Scarlet O'Hara once had a flutter
> His marriage however became quite a sham
> Because frankly my dear, he didn't give a damn.

೪

Climbing Rhyme

A Burmese poetry form, Climbing Rhyme is so called because of the repeated sequence of three internally rhymed, four syllable lines. Burmese poetry commonly has an internal rhyme rather than an end rhyme.

In this style of poetry the rhyme appears as follows:

Line 1 - in the 4th syllable

Line 2 - in the 3rd syllable

Line 3 - in the 2nd syllable

The last syllable of Line 3 commences the new rhyme for Lines 4, 5 and 6 and so on.

Often a verse ends with a higher but odd number of syllables e.g. 5, 7, 9 or 11.

The style can also be attempted by using 4 words instead of four syllables for variety.

Example: 4 syllable:

> The Owl is wise
> In night skies he
> Oft tries to snatch
> Even catch mice
> So nice to eat. Yum.

Example: 4 word

> The coal black crow
> Doesn't really know how
> To go about flight
> So hops lightly across
> Myna roads slightly bemused.

Concrete Poetry

Concrete Poetry allows the word artist to use their imagination. The aim is to write a poem that flows but one that can form a picture when end-stops are used appropriately to structure the line length. For instance, a poem about time could be written into the shape of an hour glass, a poem about an octopus can have the lines or letters running vertically to imitate tentacles. Anything is possible, as long as the words reflect the subject of the image produced.

Example

IMMIGRANT

Seconded you
came, Your home-
land left behind. Skills
in the cane field was
your fame. But alas
your stature was too
short. Of this shortfall
they hadn't thought. So
tourist adventurers you became.
South America left far behind. To conquer
our country was your aim. You visited suburbs
too I'm told. The harshness of our country did
not contain your savage push killing all within
your wake. Our toughest stance only helped you
to sustain a living; sucking water through your skin.
Round garden ponds at night - oh what a din! Our fauna
suffers dearly I confess You think that
now you're here, you're here to stay.
But we abhor your hump skinned ugliness.
Your visa is retracted, leave the bog You
revolting pop-skinned Cane Toad.
Toxic Frog!

೪

D

Diamonte

The Diamonte is very similar to the modern cinquain in that it starts with a noun, and describes the noun in several ways. The Diamonte however turns the description of the noun around to introduce a second subject that is almost a total opposite to the first. The poem consists of seven lines and should be written with the lines centred on the page so the overall image is a diamond.

a) Line 1 is one word, a noun (first subject)

b) Line 2 two adjectives describing the first subject

c) Line 3 three 'ing' verbs that describe the first subject

d) Line 4 four nouns. The first two nouns describe the first subject. The second two nouns describe a second subject that is a strong contrast to the first. The words express a feeling about the noun

e) Line 5 three 'ing' verbs describing the second subject

f) Line 6 two adjectives describing the second subject

g) Line 7 one word, a noun, the second subject.

Example:

Foal
Spindly; jughead
leg-splaying; staggering; toppling;
Innocent; yearling; gamboleer; runner
Thundering; high-blowing; striding
Shiny; elegant
Racehorse

Doditsu

The Doditsu is one of the many and varied forms of Japanese poetry. The poem consists of four lines, broken into 7-7-7-5 syllables, making a total of 26 syllables in total.

The subject of Doditsu is usually love or humour, and has no rigid metre, nor rhyme. Unlike haiku, it can be given a title.

Example:

Happy

Lines crease your face with laughter
Glee leaps into twinkling eyes
Belly, large, wriggles with mirth
Oh Master of fun.

Dylan Thomas Portrait

The Dylan Thomas Portrait gained favour amongst many noted poets after Dylan Thomas devised this short form of poetry. The poem is written in two lines, the first asking the question 'Have You Ever Seen ..' and stating a subject. The second line describes in three or four words the poet's impression of the subject.

Dylan Thomas Portraits have no title.

Example:

> Have you ever seen an artist?
> Creative, brush-minded imagineer.
>
> Have you ever seen a crocodile?
> Teeth grinning, prehistoric, death machine.
>
> Have you ever seen a hippopotamus?
> Fat waddling, wide yawning sea-cow.

E

Echo Verse

This form of poetry consists of duplicating the end words or sounds of the previous line into the following line to produce a witty or cynical response. The poem therefore consists of a long line followed by a short line. There is no limit to the length of the line or the length of the poem.

Example

Stage Echo

Player: Throng, tell me on the stage what you abhor.
Echo.   A bore.
Player: But how can I leave unspoken the lines I so adore?
Echo.   A door.
Player: But I cannot leave amid such turmoil and ado.
Echo.   Do.
Player: Oh such shame, to whom is this blame due?
Echo.   You.

Elegy

An 'elegy' is any poem written in elegiac meter (that is, alternating hexameter and pentameter lines). It can also denote the subject and mood frequently expressed in that verse form - especially complaints about love. In the Renaissance period elegies were love poems. In the 17th century they referred to poems of lament, usually about the death of a person. Elegies can also express the sorrow of the passing of human values.

The Dirge is a variation of Elegy, because it expresses grief about someone's death, but it is a shorter and much less formal poem than the elegy. A Monody is another variation and centres its focus on only one person.

Aspects that are often included in the formal elegy is that all nature joins in on the mourning; there are verbal accusations of negligence against the guardians or guardian angels of the dead; questions are raised about the justice in the event; and the mention of flowers brought to adorn the hearse. This is followed by a closing argument that supports the realisation that death has brought the passing into a higher life.

The alternating hexameter and pentameter lines form a couplet, being twelve syllables in the first line, and ten syllables in the second line. The mood is always sad and plaintive.

Example:

To the Passing Years

Oh how we solemn mourn the passing of the years
Each new change made only invokes our fears
We sad sit back and think of far better days
And how we did things in the golden ways
Oh how I miss that slow and feathered heavy tread
That lumbered by the house delivering bread
And the giggling children gathering round the cart –
The silence of the street now pains my heart.
The air we breathed back then was crystal, pure and sweet
Not like the fumy skies we constant meet
Each time we step outside. How can we survive this?
Growing old seeing lifestyle in remiss
Guardian angel, why these things did you allow?
The air, the noise is breaking sharp the bough
Of humanity. We hide inside, faces thrust
In oxygen masks, for to live we must?
Oh how I long for the long stems on my coffin
The passing parade letting me return
To the better days of an unpolluted time
When the seasons of my youth were in rhyme
When the bough of my upright tree walked tall and spread
Behind that slow and feathered heavy tread
Oh Angel of my life, I ask you, please allow
Let me walk from here behind the golden plough.

ॐ

Epigram

An epigram is a very short, and usually witty, poem or statement. It can focus on any subject, be it love, death, religion, thought, a person or event. It usually ends with a wry or dramatic twist of thought that surprises the reader.

The epigram is usually humorous, sometimes poignant, but always memorable. Its form dates back to the late 16th Century.

Example:

Mate

I tried to warn you of your imminent death
From snorting coke and drinking bottled meth.
I warned you but to die you seemed hell-bent
In party mode that is just how you went.

Ethere

The Ethere is a ten lined poem that starts with one syllable on the first line and increases one syllable in each successive line, the final line containing ten syllables.

Much fun can be had with Ethere. You can reverse the order and start with ten syllables, decreasing to one.

You can write multiple verses, reversing the order in each verse.

Example:

Giving

She
Rises
To the dawn
Feeling different
Feeling wonderful
As womanhood claims her
In his arms she'd found herself
Surrendered herself to his charms
Gave that which can never be regained
And cherished him for all eternity.

Ethere examples:

The Long Run

Flame
Of gold Flickering
On high held torch
As runners travel
The distance on sure feet
Each step taken precisely
Carrying the eternal flame
This honour bestowed never forgot
As the Olympic rings link nations.

Sweet Sounds

Sweet
birdsong
fills the air
with light floating
sound so smooth, so calm
my heart lifts, breath flows in
until my feet lift from earth
If I could trill birdsongs so sweet
Fill heart and soul with melodies pure
I'd shed the shackles from my feet and fly.

❧

Ezra Pound Couplets

Ezra Pound couplets do not have to rhyme. First introduced by poet Ezra Pound, the poem consists of two lines - the first provides a scene or image, the second provides another scene or image that is a strong comparison to the first but very different.

Example:

> Castle turrets towering on a distant hill.
> City skyline at dusk.

> Wind whipped white capped waves curling on the break
> White horses galloping to shore

F

Fabliau/Fabliaux

The Fabliaux is a short, comic or satirical tale from the 12th and 13th century medieval France and 14th century England. Usually written in eight syllable verses, they deal mainly with middle-class or lower class characters and delight in the ribald and the obscene. A favourite theme was making fun of a stupid husband.

Example: A Modern day Fabliaux

The Trouvere and the Troubadour

He walked the lands with words galore
spouting them with nuance pure
reciting epic fabliaux;
That valiant trouvere.

Composing verse he strut the land,
pen and palette in his hand;
he glorified the deeds of man,
That valiant trouvere

Until in Trouvelle Port he came
upon the Troubadour acclaimed,
of estaminet he was long fained,
That sotted Troubadour.

The Troubadour with lyre strung
attuned words of the trouvere's tongue,
these words he said he'd wrote and sung,
That sotted Troubadour.

Yet trouvere did not raise his ire,
he kowtowed low and took the lyre
and strumming strings he did aspire
to mock that Troubadour.

'Twas in the vale of Arbonné,
at close of inn on Festive day
that you, kind sir, did hear me ply
my wordsmith trade near thee.

You stole my verse, you faitor born,
I break your lyre, strung but worn,
I now redeem my work with scorn,
said valiant Trouvere.

Now scour away your sozzled name
from on my words which brought you fame;
I revoke your long attested claim
to the words of bold Trouvere.

And so the proud Trouvere did go
wandering long, reciting slow;
no more did singer steal his show,
That valiant Trouvere.

Free Form Poetry or Free Verse

Also known as 'open form', free verse does not rhyme, nor do the lines have a regular rhythm, or a regular length. Instead, lines are structured to enable the poet to manage pace, time, and place importance on a specific point or image, many single images making up the whole picture that the poet wishes the reader to see - but not just the picture - it is a series of points or glimpses that elaborate on the detail of the whole image.

The placement of words in free form poetry is very important. Placement can achieve a greater inflection on some point or other and make it strong, while allowing more flowing lines to subtly introduce a separate image within the main.

While free verse requires no rhythm or static line lengths, it should have an internal rhyme or flow within the poem.

Free verse can be produced by a technique called 'Clustering'.

To cluster, start with a word that means something special to you. Draw a circle in the centre of a piece of paper. Write that word inside the circle.

From this circle, draw arms, like the arms of an octopus. Along those lines write single statements or images about that word;

that is, what does that word make you see or think of. Go around the circle until you can think of no more.

If any statement produces a tangent thought, circle the statement and branch legs off that statement as well.

When all thoughts are exhausted, select those most poignant in your mind and write them down in a sequence that flows, so one thought flows into another. You may have to rearrange some of the lines as the poem takes shape.

Study Time

I watched a moth die this morning,
heard it first
then saw it drop from the ceiling to the shelf,
thought then it was a shame,
that its days were numbered.

I looked closer,
saw it breathing still and felt better.
Maybe it was only resting,
and pondered idly if those delicate creatures
ever really slept in their short life,
then went away to busy myself
with more important things.

I came back some time later
to engross myself in rigid print and study
and was deep within that toil
when he dropped again,
landed right before my eyes

and there he died,
took his last breath,
his final flutter,
and then was still.

I groaned
and watched him longer,
studied his dirty brown tonings;
thought that he should be an ugly thing,
yet somehow he wasn't.

That dirty brown was sheeny, silken soft,
intricately grained with black and beige,
a graphic pattern climbing and declining
along the feathery scalloped wing
foreshadowed only
by a pair of perfect peacock-tail green eyes.
And there he sat, taut before me
propped on his foreclaws
with his wings dipped to caress the ground,
poised as if ready for flight;
like a bomber on the tarmac
tensely waiting to scramble skywards
just begging for the siren to alert it,
or my hand to disturb.
So I did.

I touched it, saying
'Fly and be free, my pretty,'
but it just fell on its face, nose-dived,
the horizontal feeler prop dipping earthward,
kinking,
its sheeny wings crinkling,
its foreclaws crumpling beneath it.
And I felt sad.

I couldn't bury that moth you know –
it was much too beautiful for that,
so I put it in a matchbox
and sighed it a prayer.
Then I cursed it
for it had ruined my day
my thoughts now gone to who he was
and did he have a family that would miss him.
Poor chap.

No room for study now.
No room for more important lessons
so I left him sleeping in his matchbox on the desk
and went outside in the sunlight
to ponder Humanity and Death.

I watched a moth die this morning.

G

Ghazal

Originally developed in Persia, this form of poetry is popular in India, Pakistan and Iran, and is often put to music.

The Ghazal (pronounced g-huzzle) consists of five to fifteen couplets. The word that appears at the end of the first line, is also the terminating word of the second line in the first couplet, and the terminating word in the second line of each and every couplet thereafter.

Lines are approximately the same length and hold a similar rhythm, and before the end word one or more words rhyme or slightly rhyme. Each couplet should be an image of its own, linked only by the end word.

The final couplet usually contains the poets name in first, second or third person as they make a statement or express a feeling.

One method of titling the poem is to use the repeated end word in the title.

Example:

Peace Ghazal

Priests say: "Speak now or forever hold your peace."
So he spoke and now forever has his peace.

White birds wing across a graceful sky
The olive branch beheld, these fliers of peace.

So you cannot judge a book by its cover?
By the tattered look this must be War and Peace.

In mother's arms the infant sleeps so serene
Words can never full express their inner peace.

Helen says: "Never lie still while breath exists.
I will never lie still till I rest in peace."

H

Haiku

The Haiku is a Japanese form of poetry. The poem consists of three lines that are broken into syllables of five in the first line, seven in the second line, five in the third line, making a total of 17 syllables in all.

Traditionally the poem is about nature or reflects nature by depicting the seasons within the text in some way - that is, falling leaves imply autumn; buds imply spring; snow gives the impression of winter - yet does not actually say it is autumn, spring or winter.

Haikus should invoke the reader's senses both mentally and physically and produce a memorable picture. They should open the reader's eyes and consciousness to the world around them. The best haikus are therefore written out in the open where the poet can smell the roses, touch the budding branches, hear the crickets' serenade, bury themselves amongst long waving grasses and relate the moment to their audience as if it was happening right then, a timeless event.

The poem is always unrhymed, and has no title. Avoid using capitals and punctuation.

Examples:

burning pavements scorch
as feet march along life's road
forgive my leaping

hillside poppies weave
red carpets of memories
of wars and lost loves.

autumn scattered turf
pokes bravely through gold leaves
revealing white crosses

tiny fingers clutch hand
mother nurtures child at breast
life completes its circle

Haiku Sequence

The Haiku sequence abides by all the rules of Haiku but is a series of Haiku poems linked in a common theme. Again the sequence has no title but is referred to by the opening lines of the first haiku.

Example:

pink apple blossoms
burst forth on slender branches
bending boughs to earth

lambs frolic and grow
as seasons wend to summer
like small gentle buds

gold peeps through branches
shines up crimson winter falls
as the breeze turns cold

cold leaves drift earthward
pattern the crisp white carpet
as the season turns

Heroic couplets

Written in iambic pentameter, heroic couplets consist of two lines that are coupled together by rhyme. This poetry form makes clear-cut statements or arguments and is very economical on words. The statement or argument is completed fully in the two lines.

The poem can consist of only two lines, which is called a closed couplet, or a series of two lined stanzas which tell a story. Be careful though, a long poem in this form could easily become monotonous and lose the reader's interest.

Use couplets to say something pert and witty.

Example:

> When in your life you've teetered on the brink
> toes tipped over the edge. You turned to drink.

> Beauteous turned the earth where e'er you walked
> I felt so deep in love but then I baulked
> for all you said to make my heartstrings tied
> I found out soon enough, thank God, you lied

Heroic quatrains

Commonly used to write about heroic deeds or events, heroic quatrains are 4 lines of verse written in iambic pentameter with a rhyming scheme of abab. This form is also known as an 'elegiac' stanza as it can be used to write elegies.

Heroic couplets and quatrains can be used in the writing of narrative poems but again, they can become difficult to read if the poem is long because the metre becomes boring, and the rhyme becomes too repetitious for the enjoyment to be sustained for long.

Example:

The Lion Roars

On fess and par the rampant lion stands
his golden mane like kingdom's banner
waves
as Lordship rides the ruler of his land
while bowing at his feet his knights and naves

The Holy Wars became his tryst, his lust
his knights beside him rode on these
Crusades
but on the battlefield, they all were lost
and their names from memory forever fades

❧

I

Idyll

An idyll is a form of lyrical verse that paints a picture of some simple type of life, generally rural, but it is always written in a way that idealises the image. The romantic idyll paints a picture of the days of chivalry. This song of joy about a scene or some aspect of nature is usually brief and rhymes but can also be written in free form.

Example: Free form

Morning in Terrington

Mists hang low over darkened dew-kissed ground
as cows, like black and white Picassos, amble slow
heads down, on the cobbled roads and
swards of border green they trudge towards the sheds
Horses lift their moistened heads
stretch over stony fences
Nicker soft at the passing ritual.

They breathe, and shrouds of white increase, swirls
where willows drip long fingers to the pond
a cat, striped tabby, slinks from the milking shed
as greyness peels from its bed like silken sheets
and sparrows spread their wings
as the sun fingers her way beneath the clouds
 morning cometh as ghostly shadows lift
and white milk flows inside the shed.

Example: Rhyming

Morning

Pink clouds daub a silken sky
pierced by rainbow arching down
It touches earth on velvet rye
'tween grazing cows of white and brown.

Green velvet waves in zephyr's light
that wafts aside the chiffon mists
as red breasts puff their chests so bright
and drink their fill of dewdrops kiss.

Beyond the field shines sunbeams gold
that fingers gently across the scene
light the wheels so ancient, old
of dray that once so young had been.

I feel my days of youthfulness
are passing soon and I must fade
and leave this land where I was blest
and seasons revelled as I played.

The mists have gone, the pink clouds drift
the rainbow fades as does my time
On satin scene my memories sift
of this land, this life, all gems sublime.

❧

J

Jabberwocky

This is a really fun stuff, a style of poetry loosely termed Jabberwocky as it duplicates the famous poem from 'Alice Through the Looking Glass' by Lewis Carroll. It can be classed Macaronic Verse, Nonsense Verse or Portmanteau. Your attempt could be titled 'A Parody of Jabberwocky' as some of the lines from Jabberwocky are duplicated in total.

Acquire and analyse the poem 'Jabberwocky', and refer to the Portmanteau listing on page 8 to learn how to develop suitable words. The important thing is to write jibberish yet still have the reader using their imagination to picture something happening. A story indeed unfolds from the non- existent words.

Stanza Rules:

1. Commence the poem with 'Twas.

   The rest of the quatrain is your choice but remember it will be repeated in full as the last stanza

2. The lines are

   "Beware the (something - 2 syllables) my son!

   The jaws that bite, the claws that catch.

   Beware the (a different something) and shun The .... (yet another something)."

3. Lines are

   He took his (something - 2 words) in hand

   Long time the (something) foe he sought

So rested he by the (something) tree

And stood a while in thought.

4. Lines are

And, as in (something) thought he stood

The (first something from stanza 2) with eyes of flame

Came (something - action) through the (something)

And (something - action) as it came.

5. Lines are

One two! One two! And through and through

The (something from stanza three first line - 2 words) went (something - 2 words).

He left it dead, and with its head

He went (something - action - 3 syllables) back.

6. Lines are

"And hast though slain the (something - from line 1 stanza 2)

Come to my arms you (something - 2 syllables) boy"

Third line exultant words of own choice

He chortled in his joy.

7. Repeat stanza one in total.

Jabberwocky is a great way to spend some idle moments, and a great party activity where writers are present.

Example:

Trackerwocky

'Twas sprungly and the glyty golts
did rolt and gallock on the guff
all prantled were the stalliolts
and the millies chit the duff.

Beware the Champiock, my son
the jaws that bite, the claws that catch
beware the Racetard, and shun
the frazzled Race Dispatch.

He took his Stooters gud in hand
Long time the barrigate he sought
So rested he by the Lookout tree
And stood a while in thought

And as in awpal thought he stood
The Champiock, with eyes of flame
Came strincing through the melleecowd
And squortled as it came.

One, Two! One Two! And through and through
The Stooters gud went boom and clack
He left it dead and with its head
He went chareelling back

And has though slain the Champiock
Come to my arms, you boobling boy
Oh bleeding miff and paddawhack
He chortled in his joy?

'Twas sprungly and the glyty golts
did rolt and gallock on the guff
all prantled were the stalliolts
and the millies chit the duff.

K

Kyrielle

A French form of rhyming poetry, the Kyrielle is written in four line stanzas (quatrain) with each stanza containing a repeated line or phrase (usually the last line but not essentially so). Each line consists strictly of eight syllables. Three stanzas is considered the minimum with no maximum length applied to the form.

Popular rhyming schemes are:

a) aabB, ccbB, ddbB,

B is the refrain or repeated line, or

b) abaB, cbcB, dbdB.

B is the refrain or repeated line

The rhyming scheme however is the poet's choice.

Example:

Tears in the Sea

Deep in my dreams you call my name
I come to you, much to my shame
for we no more can ever be
my tears flow freely to the sea

Once life was good, my life was blest
we loved and frolicked in the mist
you stole my heart, you had the key
now my tears flow freely to the sea

And now I sleep with endless dreams
your plans were not as mine it seems
as I live my life in agony
my tears flow freely to the sea.

L

Lantern/Lanturne

Similar to a cinquain, the Lantern consists of five lines, each line based on the number of syllables per line. As with the cinquain, the first and last lines should be words that mean the same or at least have a strong connection.

a) Line One consists of one syllable

b) Line Two consists of two syllables

c) Line Three consists of three syllables

d) Line Four consists of four syllables

e) Line Five consists of one syllable that relates to or means the same as the first line.

The shape formed by the poem resembles a Japanese lantern

Examples:

Satin
Sheets slide
Lovers out
In the open
Sprung

Screen
Cursor
prompts action
prompts action now!
Work

Limerick

The Limerick is a traditional old favourite that consists of five lines and usually started with 'There was a ......' but doesn't have to. They should always be humorous or quirky.

The Limerick contains:

Eight beats in the first line,

Eight beats in the second line

Five beats in the third line,

Five beats in the fourth line, Eight beats in the last line.

Lines 1, 2 and 5 rhyme together, Lines 3 and 4 rhyme together.

The Limerick is one of the hardest poems to write. It is usually the last line that is the hardest to achieve.

Examples:

There was an old lady from Rome
who travelled quite often alone
She went saw the Pope
who thought her a dope
said: "you should buy a mobile phone."

A young miss from Hamlet went fishing
to catch a young man she was wishing
she cast out her line
and reeled him in fine
but then noticed her man net was missing

M

Mono-rhyme

The Mono-rhyme can be a difficult poem to write because the essence of the poem is not only to tell a story or depict an image, but to also rhyme the end word in every line. The secret of successful mono-rhyme poetry is to make your first end word one that has many rhyming possibilities.

There is no set meter or line length, no restriction on subject matter, no defined stanza length or line limit.

Example:

Redemption

Over the dunes of white soft sand
The woman comes to make her stand
Scorned by kith and shunned by man
She makes her stand.

Down the dune to white wet sand
The woman pads to make her stand
Seethes at kith and vengeful of man
She makes her stand.

Below the dunes on wet white sand
The woman wades to make her stand
Wrath at kith and scornful of man
She makes her stand.

Beyond the dunes and white soft sand
The woman sinks; can no longer stand
Guilt to kith and accusing man
She's made her stand.

Mono-tetra

A variation of the Mono-rhyme is the Mono-tetra, a new form of poetry developed by poet Michael Walker.

The poem is divided into quatrains. Each line in the stanza rhymes, giving a rhyming scheme of aaaa.

There are eight syllables in each line (or four beats) until the last stanza line which has two sets of four syllables (two beats), and a repetition of the same four syllables to make four beats.

There is no limit to the number of stanzas in a Mono-tetra.

Example:

Changing Patterns

She started with a baby toy
soon progressed to gigolo boy
at first she was extremely coy
but found what joy! But found what joy!

She found a boy to idolise
he caught her heart with such surprise
they lay in arms until sunrise
Oh what a prize! Oh what a prize!

But into love came love's cruel twist
Gigolo boy sadly remised
it seemed that love did not exist
A harmless tryst? A harmless tryst?

She didn't know how she would cope
through every day she'd sadly mope
but then he phoned which gave her hope
Kaleidoscope! Kaleidoscope!

N

Naani

Originating in India, the Naani consists of 4 lines that have a total of 20 to 25 syllables, with no set manner in the distribution. Subject matter is open, though generally touches on human factors, such as emotions, thought, and human behaviour.

Examples:

> Loose the noose
> on the growing child
> and place trust in all
> you have taught them over the years

> Eccentricity
> is the art of being capricious
> being capricious
> is fanciful.

Nonet

The nonet is similar to the reversed Ethere, except that it contains only nine lines. There are nine syllables in the first line, eight in the second line, seven in the third line and so on, until the last line which contains a single syllable.

Nonets can be written on any subject, and may or may not rhyme.

Example:

Lonely Island

On a distant shore we look to sea
hand in hand we stand, you and I
the rat race left far behind
as we search for a place
an island of hope.
Marooned, we are
so alone
stranded.
Yes!!

∾

O

Ode

This is a truly classical form of poetry. An ode has no fixed stanza form or verse pattern. It is usually longish, but contains less than a hundred lines. It can be rhymed or unrhymed - unrhymed being rarer. It is lyrical, that is, it is poetic, romantic, emotional, inspiring, expressive.

Generally an ode presents an image or scene and speculates or comments on the exact nature or character of that image or scene. Deep meaning is usually placed on the picture painted, and it should be obvious that there is great intimacy between the poet and the subject.

Traditionally, odes were sung.

Example:

Ode to a Poet

Outward pourings from the mind inspire
as words upon the page a picture paint
the images so real my heart doth fire
the places that he writes I reacquaint
for he hath made the scenes appear so real
daubed turquoise on a cotton candy cloud
made palm trees sway beside a golden beach
I see my land, and ever I am proud
while bubbling brook with silver glints reveal
the music that I played there and I feel
the poet placed my homeland in my reach

He does not know the things he makes me feel
Nor understands the wonders that I see
for his the words of mind he has to deal
from where they come is still a mystery
He has no knowledge of the place I know
his words so magical pour on the page
ripe and stored in mind they flow like wine
the reader's heart to mellow and engage
and as I read my heart begins to glow
warm tears touch my eyes and start to flow
for the poet's heart is rich and so divine.

Ottava Rima

A style not often used these days, Ottava Rima is an Italian form of poetry that has eight lines and a rhyming scheme of

a b a b a b c c.

It is written in iambic tetrameter (8 syllable), pentameter (10 syllable), or hendecasyllables (11 syllable) lines. The style was usually used by satirists as the rhyming scheme enabled them to split rhyme and use enjambment to impress points as needed.

The Rime Royal discussed in later pages was developed from the Ottava Rima, Ottava Rima being the longer form.

Example:

Birdsong

Oh sweet the sound that ripples through the trees
That lights the heart and takes all cares away
The music sweet is carried on the breeze
At eventide it murmurs with the grey
At night it soulful sings soliloquies
While birds await the dawning of the day
My birdsong choir never fails to thrill
I lay, eyes closed, and listen to it still.

❧

P

Pantoum

A Malayan form of poetry, the Pantoum consists of quatrains of unlimited number, line length and metre.

Lines 2 and 4 of the first stanza become lines 1 and 3 of the second stanza, repeated in their entirety and with as little modification as possible.

Lines 2 and 4 of the second stanza become lines 1 and 3 of the third stanza, and so on.

To finish, the last stanza consists of lines 1 and 3 of the first stanza, positioned as either lines 1 and 2 but preferably as lines 2 and 4, with line 3 being placed before line 1 so that the first line of the poem is the last line of the poem.

This is similar to the French Villanelle. (See page 147)

Hint: Any easy way to write Pantoum is to number your lines 1 to 16, then write your first stanza. Next, position lines 2 and 4 into the next stanza before adding the new lines to it. Then position lines 2 and 4 from the second stanza into the third stanza and write the new lines of stanza three, and so on.

Example:

Priceless

At some stage he realised it wasn't his day
The CPR pummel was four minutes late
He stared at the heaven's from where he lay
Disappointed that this was his fate.

The CPR pummel was four minutes late
His mate at his side knew not what to do
Disappointed that this was his fate
He gasped till his lips turned blue

His mate at his side knew not what to do
When he fell to the floor in total surprise
He gasped till his lips turned blue
That the Lotto win was solely his prize.

When he fell to the floor in total surprise
He stared at the heaven's from where he lay
Not a nickel he spent of his total cash prize
At that stage he realized it wasn't his day.

Paradelle

A fixed form of French poetry dating back to the 11th Century, the Paradelle consists of four stanzas of six lines with a repetitive pattern placed rigidly throughout.

Line 1 is repeated in its entirety as Line 2. Line 3 is repeated in its entirety as Line 4.

Now this is where it gets difficult. Line 5 and 6 must use all the words of Line 1 and 3, using every word only once to complete two new lines to the stanza.

Stanzas two and three are patterned the same.

The final stanza causes the most headaches because the poet must use every word in the previous three stanzas (being lines 5, 6, 11, 12, 17 & 18) once to form six new lines without repetition. Rhyming end lines give the poem a nice rounding off, but it is not essential to do so.

There is also no set line length or meter to this form opening it to a wide range of subjects.

Hint: Use solid words and limit conjunctions and pronouns. Some internal rhymes in the lines also offers greater choice of end rhymes.

W rite each word on a small blank piece of paper so the words can be shuffled around till a sensible combination is reached.

Example:

Paradelle of Dreams

Night train ferry my dreams away
Night train ferry my dreams away
Dreams by day bring streams of tears
Dreams by day bring streams of tears
My dreams of night ferry by streams
Bring tears away, train day dreams.

Along the steel wheels murmur long
Along the steel wheels murmur long
Carries the pain I feel away
Carries the pain I feel away
Wheels murmur along the steel
Carries away the long pain I feel.

I lay long hours fighting dreams of you
I lay long hours fighting dreams of you
Praying the train will take me away
Praying the train will take me away
Long hours you take me, I will lay
Fighting, praying the train of dreams away.

Long train carries my dreams away
Hours of fighting dreams of the day
By streams murmur wheels I will feel
Praying I lay along the steel
Dreams bring tears, you ferry away the pain
Take me long away, night train.

Parallelismus Membrorum

Of Hebrew origin, Parallislismus Membrorum have a history steeped in religion, in fact they are present in the Old Testament. Modern poets however have used this style to reflect on self or how self links with nature.

The lines, called members, are parallel in structure and subject. Each line usually contains no more than three or four words. If the first line has four words, then all lines have four words. Poems are usually short in length - from two lines but not often more than eight lines.

Parallelisms can be formed in the following ways:

a) Synonymous parallelisms

The first line expresses a sentiment or thought. The second line expresses the same thought or sentiment in different words. The poem can consist of two or three statements linked in common thought.

b) Antithetical parallelisms

The first line expresses a sentiment or thought, the second line expresses an opposite viewpoint. The poem continues for two or three synonymous statements that are countered in the interim lines.

c) Synthetical parallesisms

The first line expresses an idea or feeling. Its counter line expresses a very different idea yet is strongly connected to the first in some way.

Example: Antithetical

Ply me with riches
Clothe me in rags
I am the prophet
I see no future
Doors open for me
Slam the door shut
I am goodness profound
The devil I am.

Parody

A Parody is written by taking a well-known poem or song, using the same rhythms and metres but rewriting the words to produce a humorous outcome. Much fun can be gained from writing parodies.

Try rewriting nursery rhymes, Christmas Carols, well known poems and pop songs.

Example: Nursery Rhymes

> Ride a cross horse to incite its toss
> Till it sheds the fine lady - oh what a loss
> With breaks in her fingers, no brains in her head
> I shall now have to cure her with two ounces of lead.

Example: Song

Heartburn

(To the tune 'Heartache')

Heartburn, Heartburn,
your cooking always gives me Heartburn
I took a Quickeze just the other day
I had another now, I had one yesterday

Heartburn, Heartburn
Why do you always give me heartburn?
I sent you to a class in cookery
How is it still that food's a burning memory?

Heartburn, Heartburn
I'm sure you work to give me heartburn
I tried another cure the other day
I found your cooking best
From at least two miles away

Heartburn, Heartburn
I know you love to give me heartburn
Today I found out the best cure yet
It's called divorce, you bet!

❧

Prose Poetry

Prose Poetry is very much at first appearance a chunk of prose with very carefully placed end stops. What differentiates it from pure prose is the depth of emotion and the word-ology used - that is, the use of very descriptive phrases to produce a vivid picture in the shortest possible way, or the dramatic inflection produced by the mere placement of words.

Try writing a descriptive piece of prose on a subject you feel strongly about. Look at the piece you have written and break it into phrases, each phrase producing an image of its own. The combined 'line images' come together to produce the whole story or dramatic impression.

Example:

Today

You yell – "NO WAR!"
"Bring our Troops home!"
Taunt the USA with cries
Wave banners
that call them Ruthless Invaders
They have no right!

I think of brown skinned Iraquis
The academic Kurds
The lost families of Halabja,
    cuddled together in the streets,
    died where they fell, breathing fake air –
    senseless slaughter.
The crushed and crippled of New York

Our own peace-loving revellers of Bali
The brain-washed suicide bombers -
   dying for Allah
   dying for Hussein
   dying for Bin Laden
Which God?
Promises of riches for the death of a few

I think of oppression
A dictator's rule
Portraits towering on every corner
I think of the three hundred students
   taken from Baghdad College
disappeared after misconstrued statements
I think of the senselessness of future planning
   - might not be here tomorrow -
and fears of walking safe on our streets
speaking without fear of reprisal
from governmentary spies.

And I say -
"Go get 'em boys!"
The world will be a better place
for this is our War –
A war of Freedom for us and the Iraquis.

∿

Q

Quatern

This French form of poetry, similar to the Kyrielle, consists of four quatrains, each line containing eight syllables. There is no specific metre or rhyming scheme to be maintained but a refrain exists that is repeated in a new position in each new quatrain.

Line 1 in the first quatrain moves to line 2 in the second quatrain, to line 3 in the third quatrain and to the last line in the fourth quatrain.

Subject matter is open.

Example:

Leaving

The wind blows through me like a prayer
As clouds float by so ethereal
My past is drifting on the air,
What's this sensation that I feel?

I cannot comprehend just why
The wind blows through me like a prayer;
But breath releases as a sigh
And takes my memories to the air

My memories float without a care
And swirl around me on the breeze
The wind blows through me like a prayer
And I for once feel so at ease.

I give myself as I'm beset
And meet my Lord without a care
My life is done. With faith I let
The wind blow through me like a prayer.

Quatrain

As mentioned previously, a quatrain is a four line stanza. There are numerous poetic forms that incorporate quatrains in their structure: sonnets, rubayaits, ballads, and lyrical verse, to name a few.

Common rhyming schemes for a quatrain are:

a)   abcb

b)   abba

c)   abab

d)   aabb

e)   abca

f)   aaab

g)   abac

Example:

Sublimity

I stand and watch gold grasses blow
Wave 'neath the sky wind's ebb and flow
Quilting the landscape, sown by hand
Human sustenance raised from the land.

Ears prick tall as I pass by their stance
Lay slightly o'er as my horse's feet dance
My hand lightly glides over feelers so fine
To know I have raised this is truly sublime.

From o'er the next pasture comes minimal bleat
As lambs white and fluffy come to their feet
Their mumma's protective stamp hard the ground
Stirs the flock harshly to gather around.

Wool deep and weathered the rams raise their
heads
I draw rein on the bridle and watch how we tread
Not to disturb them, their cottonball play
We rein to the right and move soon away.

Through seasons of sunlight and seasons of wet
I think fond of memories I cannot forget
Across this great land I full cherish my time
The life of a farmer is truly sublime.

Quinzaine

The Quinzaine is a three lined poem consisting of fifteen syllables. The syllables are arranged seven syllables in the first line, five in the second and three in the third. The lines are unrhymed.

Line one makes a statement.

Lines 2 and 3 ask questions relating to the statement in line one. Remember the syllable count.

Example:

> Hello Guardian Angel!!
> Are you an angel?
> Do you guard?

ℰ

R

Renga

Renga can be a game between poets or can be written solo. The art of Renga is to link your thoughts to the preceding verse, and only to the preceding verse. Renga means 'linked verse', ren meaning linked because verses are linked by subject matter and thought, and ga meaning elegance.

There are many types of renga, each type having its own set of rules, which are rigidly set. The combination of all stanzas makes the whole composition.

Evolved from the Tanka, Renga has a beginning, middle and an ending. The opening verse is called the hokku, which is usually the privilege of the host or the most experienced renga writer to deliver. After that each stanza is written by alternating poets, unless otherwise indicated in the rules.

It is wise to decide on the theme or purpose of the poem and the subjects it will touch to avoid the Renga becoming too abstract to hold meaning.

Decide what the hokku will reflect. Which season will provide the opening scene? Will it make reference to the group and their reason for writing the poem? All this happens in the first three lines.

The jo or introduction is contained in the first six stanza which are strongly linked. This part of the poem is quite business-like as the poets get to know each other - in the Japanese way this is a polite introduction.

The next 24 links reveal the relationship growing between the poets, as they use their words and images to strengthen their relationship and jump from subject to subject or debate an issue in words. As the mind leaps and twists the images to set up subsequent stanzas so the intrigue of the poem grows. Each new set of lines links only to the set of lines preceding it.

The last six stanzas are the closure, where all that has occurred in the previous 24 links is ratified, rectified and reflected on, and links the poem back to the hokku.

There are rules to be aware of during the construction of Renga:

There should be a fair mixture of nature and human affairs and the more pleasant seasons. Subjects raised should not be repeated, and nor should nouns and adjectives once introduced - once the name or subject is mentioned it should not be mentioned again.

Capitals and punctuation are usually avoided.

The seasons are depicted by image rather than by stipulating winter, summer, autumn, spring. Non-seasonal images usually relate to human affairs, people or places.

Follow the set pattern for the Renga style chosen, writing in alternating patterns of 3 lines then 2 lines. The title is taken from the first link, and the authors names are listed under the title.

Winter Kasen Renga

Verse	Content Mentioned

Opening

1. A haiku of 5-7-5 syllables about winter. Written by the first poet or host.

2. 2 lines about winter, 7 syllables each line. Links to the first verse. Written by the second poet

3. 3 lines that are non-seasonal and should end in a verb by the first or third poet

4. 2 lines non-seasonal

5. 3 lines. Must mention the moon and autumn in some way.

6. 2 lines mentioning autumn.

Middle

7. The poet of verse #6 also writes this verse. 3 lines mentioning autumn.

8. 2 lines, non-seasonal. A love verse.

9. 3 lines, non-seasonal. A love verse.

10. 2 lines, non-seasonal. A love verse.

11. 3 lines, non-seasonal

12. 2 lines, non-seasonal

13. 3 lines mentioning summer and the moon

14. 2 lines mentioning summer

15. 3 lines, non-seasonal

16. 2 lines, non-seasonal

17. 3 lines, mentioning a flower and spring

18. 2 lines mentioning spring

19. 3 lines mentioning spring, written by the poet who wrote verse #18

20. 2 lines, non-seasonal

21. 3 lines, non-seasonal

22. 2 lines, non-seasonal

23. 3 lines, mentioning winter

24. 2 lines, mentioning winter

25. 3 lines, non-seasonal, love verse

26. 2 lines, non-seasonal, love verse

27. 3 lines, non-seasonal, love verse

28. 2 lines, non-seasonal

29. 3 lines, mentioning the moon and autumn

30. 2 lines, mentioning autumn

Ending

31. 3 lines, mentioning autumn, written by the poet of verse #30

32. 2 lines, non-seasonal

33. 3 lines, non-seasonal

34. 2 lines, non-seasonal/spring

35. 3 lines, mentioning a flower and spring

36. 2 lines, mentioning spring that links to verse #1 in a way that closes the poem.

Spring Kasen Renga

Special Rules: Do not use the word 'woman', and if mentioned, use the words 'dreams' and 'insects' only once. The title is taken from the hokku, and the authors' names are listed directly beneath it.

Verse   Content Mentioned

Opening

1. A haiku of 5-7-5 syllables about spring. Written by the first poet or host.

2. 2 lines about spring, 7 syllables each line. Links to the first verse. Written by the second poet

3. 3 lines mentioning spring, written by the first or third poet

4. 2 lines non-seasonal

5. 3 lines. Must mention the moon and autumn in some way.

6. 2 lines mentioning autumn.

Middle

7. The poet of verse #6 also writes this verse. 3 lines mentioning autumn.

8. 2 lines, non-seasonal. A love verse.

9. 3 lines, non-seasonal. A love verse.

10. 2 lines, non-seasonal. A love verse.

11. 3 lines, non-seasonal

12. 2 lines, non-seasonal

13. 3 lines mentioning summer and the moon

14. 2 lines mentioning summer

15. 3 lines mentioning summer

16. 2 lines, non-seasonal

17. 3 lines, mentioning a flower and spring

18. 2 lines mentioning spring

19. 3 lines mentioning spring, written by the poet who wrote verse #18

20. 2 lines, non-seasonal

21. 3 lines, non-seasonal

22. 2 lines, non-seasonal

23. 3 lines, mentioning winter

24. 2 lines, mentioning winter

25. 3 lines, non-seasonal, love verse

26. 2 lines, non-seasonal, love verse

27. 3 lines, non-seasonal, love verse

28. 2 lines, non-seasonal

29. 3 lines, mentioning the moon and autumn

30. 2 lines, mentioning autumn

Ending

31. 3 lines, mentioning autumn, written by the poet of verse #30

32. 2 lines, non-seasonal

33. 3 lines, non-seasonal

34. 2 lines, non-seasonal

35. 3 lines, mentioning a flower and spring

36. 2 lines, mentioning spring, and links to verse #1 to close the poem.

Summer Kasen Renga

The title is taken from the first link, and the authors names are listed under the title.

Verse   Content Mentioned

Opening

1. A haiku of 5-7-5 syllables about summer. Written by the first poet or host.

2. 2 lines about summer, 7 syllables each line. Links to the first verse. Written by the second poet

3. 3 lines, non-seasonal, written by the first or third poet

4. 2 lines non-seasonal

5. 3 lines. Must mention the moon and autumn in some way.

6. 2 lines mentioning autumn.

Middle

7. The poet of verse #6 also writes this verse. 3 lines mentioning autumn.

8. 2 lines, non-seasonal. A love verse.

9. 3 lines, non-seasonal. A love verse.

10. 2 lines, non-seasonal. A love verse.

11. 3 lines, non-seasonal

12. 2 lines, non-seasonal

13. 3 lines mentioning winter and the moon

14. 2 lines mentioning winter

15.   3 lines, non-seasonal

16.   2 lines, non-seasonal

17.   3 lines, mentioning a flower and spring

18.   2 lines mentioning spring

19.   3 lines mentioning spring, written by the poet who wrote verse #18

20.   2 lines, non-seasonal

21.   3 lines, non-seasonal

22.   2 lines, non-seasonal

23.   3 lines, mentioning summer

24.   2 lines, mentioning summer

25.   3 lines, non-seasonal, love verse

26.   2 lines, non-seasonal, love verse

27.   3 lines, non-seasonal, love verse

28.   2 lines, non-seasonal

29.   3 lines, mentioning the moon and autumn

30.   2 lines, mentioning autumn

Ending

31.   3 lines, mentioning autumn, written by the poet of verse #30

32.   2 lines, non-seasonal

33.   3 lines, non-seasonal

34.   2 lines, non-seasonal/spring

35.   3 lines, mentioning a flower and spring

36.   2 lines, mentioning spring, and links to verse #1 to close.

Autumn Kasen Renga

The title is taken from the hokku, and the authors names are listed under the title. Verse   Content Mentioned

Opening

1.   A haiku of 5-7-5 syllables about autumn. Written by the first poet or host.

2.   2 lines about the moon, 7 syllables each line. Links to the first verse. Written by the second poet

3.   3 lines, non-seasonal, written by the first or third poet

4.   2 lines non-seasonal

5.   3 lines, mentioning winter.

6.   2 lines mentioning winter.

Middle

7.   The poet of verse #6 also writes this verse. 3 lines mentioning autumn.

8.   2 lines, non-seasonal. A love verse.

9.   3 lines, non-seasonal. A love verse.

10.   2 lines, non-seasonal. A love verse.

11.   3 lines, non-seasonal

12.   2 lines, non-seasonal

13.   3 lines mentioning the moon and summer OR winter

14.   2 lines mentioning summer OR winter

15.   3 lines, mentioning summer OR winter

16.   2 lines, non-seasonal

17. 3 lines, mentioning a flower and spring

18. 2 lines mentioning spring

19. 3 lines mentioning spring, written by the poet who wrote verse #18

20. 2 lines, non-seasonal

21. 3 lines, non-seasonal

22. 2 lines, non-seasonal

23. 3 lines, mentioning summer OR winter

24. 2 lines, mentioning summer OR winter

25. 3 lines, non-seasonal, love verse

26. 2 lines, non-seasonal, love verse

27. 3 lines, non-seasonal, love verse

28. 2 lines, non-seasonal

29. 3 lines, mentioning the moon and autumn

30. 2 lines, mentioning autumn

Ending

31. 3 lines, mentioning autumn, written by the poet of verse #30

32. 2 lines, non-seasonal

33. 3 lines, non-seasonal

34. 2 lines, non-seasonal / spring

35. 3 lines, mentioning a flower and spring

36. 2 lines, mentioning spring, and links to verse #1 to close the poem.

Renga Variation – Ninjuin Renga

The Ninjuin Renga contains only 20 verses and is an ideal starting point for new renga poets. As in all Renga the verses must link to the verse that precedes and follows, and must stand alone as an independent image.

As in all Renga, there is reference to a season in the hokku and the Renga moves through the seasons, in any order, to end with a verse on spring. Each verse must link briefly and move on, producing images without repetition of image, word or phrase.

The Ninjuin Renga is divided into three stages of opening (4 verses), middle (12 verses) and ending (4 verses). Some stipulations should be adhered to, such as:

The moon should be referred to in verse #3

A flower should be mentioned in verse #19

A Love theme appears somewhere through the poem and is sustained for three verses.

Ninjuin Renga is far less rigid that other Renga forms with the emphasis placed on mood, linking verses and moving on, and maintaining a haiku-like format with brief but descriptive images.

Example: Solo Spring Kasen Renga

Continuum

hazy arched spectrum
standing at the rainbow's end
colours misty ponds

crop arms quiver in light breeze
slow rising fields gleam morning

feather footed foals
gambol on wide sweeping plains
pick at new sweet shoots

swish-tails kick up heels in jest
laughter roils the babbling brook

falling leaves tumble
scatter 'neath night's yellow face
clouds cover bright stars

gentle blow the russet falls
denuded stands of maple

crispness chills the air
as waves dance on foggy seas
salt lingers on lips

dolphins mime aqua ballet
bond beneath the turquoise deep

adoration grows
vibrant hearts burst full of pride
hand and lips join

careful choose the path
no returns from tomorrow
bid all happiness

take the thin road overgrown
much excitement will prevail

tread wary on time
long the marks remain in snow
bitter the memories

daytime galoshes tip-toe
kick ice maidens from pickets

mother and daughter
stroll hand in hand contented
window shopping poor

kitten capers captivate
pretend tigers behind glass

long grasses divide
giggles drift on unkempt swards
sisters in rhyme

gems of reflections nurtured
carry pearls into old age

September songs lull
leaves cascade as lovers walk
romantic moonglow

southbound wings fill morning sky
children tussle in leaf piles

fate lays on the table bared
kismetic exposition

picture cards reveal possibilities of life
deal out the future

wisdom jingles like gold coins
rattles against a sad heart

night of nights draws near
sky's spectres play overhead tag
as day lingers long

stalks stand rigid on cracked earth
heat shimmers invoke their wave

fires crackle cruelly
consumes God's gift with red tongue
blackens azure skies

mouth spouts hot words of sheer spite
do naught to provoke their heat

apple blossom buds
weigh down splendid orchard boughs
honey nectar drips

birds twitter in nests high up
the air is filled with fragrance

verdant patchworks stretch
basking beneath perfect blue skies
dragonflies tango

regale in pleasance of life
dwell not on where it takes you
solace in grey sheets

overhead promises rain
crisp clean streets again

garbage disposal clatters
electronic arms deform

suburban stench drifts
hearsay infiltrates time's space
gossip mongering

retreat behind lace curtains
deniance of everything

precious moments snatched
wisteria hangs lithe
purple emotions

a coat of many colours
haloes the earth, space and time.

Rictameter

The Rictameter is similar to the traditional Cinquain where the first line contains two syllables and you build each line by increasing by two syllables. In the Rictameter you continue increasing until ten syllables is achieved, then the poem turns and decreases by two syllables each line until you get back to two syllables. Those two syllables are the original two that started the poem.

Example:

Winter
bitter winter
settles on bending boughs
making the landscape white and soft
swirling fairy floss flurries down the street
In the yard children make snowmen
Jack Frost pane dances
How I adore
Winter

❧

Rime Royal

Introduced by Chaucer, the Rime Royal is a seven line stanza that has a rhyming scheme of:

a b a b b c c (in its traditional form).

A narrative style poem, it is written in iambic pentameter.

More modern usage also accepts the following rhyming schemes:

a)   a b a b c b c

b)   a b b a b c c

c)   a b b a a c c

Example:

Ornamental

Upon the wall it takes a special place
I hung it there and rightful so it seems
for on the wall the catcher starts to chase
and gather for my keeping all my dreams.
In dark of night, I dance upon moonbeams
I love that in my heart my dreams renew
kept by Dream Catcher and my thoughts of you.

Rondeau

Originating in the 14th and 15th Century, this French form of poetry has stayed very much intact for over 200 years.

The traditional form consists of four stanzas, the first and last stanzas being identical. The second half of the second stanza is a short refrain which is the first part of the first line.

The earliest Rondeau had stanzas of two or three lines, later in the 15th Century stanzas of four, five or six lines were not uncommon.

In modern times it is usual to have 13 lines with only two rhymes - 15 lines if the refrain lines are counted - broken into a quintet (a stanza of five lines) and quatrain (4 lines) and a sestet (6 lines).

The refrain is the first half of the opening line and is repeated at the ends of the second and third stanzas, added after the 8th and 13th lines.

The Rhyming Scheme is:

A a b b a   a a b R   a a b b a R (R being Refrain).

Each line is usually 8 syllables.

Example:

Juan's Dream

Wild stallions on the hills run free
where land rolls far as the eye can see
And me, I long to join their plight
galloping through those hills at night
Such companions we would be

And - I confess - but can't
foresee
a plan of sheer debauchery
of plundering mares to our delight
Wild stallions on the hill.

If we could prance across the lea
The stallions wild and wild heart me
Hearts would break at the mere
sight
of our presence in the night.

Oh how I long this dream would be
Wild stallions on the hill.

Rondel

The Rondel is another form of French verse. It consists of 13 lines, or 14 lines if the second line is repeated at the end.

To be truly accurate the poem is divided into three stanzas. Lines one and two are the same as lines seven and eight and the same as 13 and 14 (if 14 is used).

The rhyming scheme is   abba abab abbaa (b)

Modern Rondel can be as follows:

One stanza of four lines and one stanza of five or six lines.

The first two lines are repeated as a refrain in the seventh and eighth lines and again in the 13th and 14th lines.

Example:

In Dreams I Fly

Like a soaring gull I fly in dreams
Feel I've clasped the world within my hand
feel your heart is mine forever to command
I've achieved my precious goals, it seems

O'er hills and vales, lakes and streams
my power sweeps over all the land
like a soaring gull, I fly in dreams
feel I've clasped the world within my hand

And while I fly my senses gleam
it seems that I have made my stand
faced demons that I conquered, and
like a soaring gull, I fly in dreams
feel I've clasped the world within my hand

Rondelet

The Rondelet is a brief French verse form with a refrain that generally consists of two or more words but can be the whole of the first line. Whatever the format, the refrain is half the metre/beats as the remaining lines e.g. if the refrain is four syllables, the remaining lines are eight syllables.

The Rondelet has five lines, (seven counting the refrain). Two rhymes are maintained in the one stanza.

The rhyming Scheme is:

A (=R) b R a b b R

Example:

As I Grow Old

As I grow old
your memory with me stays
as I grow old
I treat my thoughts of you like gold
for I loved you, dear, in so many ways
I treasure all our nights and days
as I grow old.

Rubaiyat

Robaiyat is Persian for quatrain, the plural of which is Robai. Rubaiyat is Arabic for quatrain, the plural being Rubai. (Rubá means four).

Therefore this form of poetry, Arabic or Persian, relies on a quatrain to make a complete statement. Line length or metre is usually tetrameter (8 syllables or 4 beats) or pentameter (10 syllables or 5 beats.)

The rhyming scheme is aaba.

It is permissible to interlock Rubaiyat by writing a series of quatrains where the rhyming scheme of the first quatrain influences the rhyming scheme of the second quatrain and so on.

It is done as follows:

Aaba

Bbcb

Ccdc

Dded

Example:

Rubiayat of Unrequited Love

I'd like to walk a mile in your shoes
To delve into the reason for your blues
I'd strive to shed the camel from your back
And why you pay so harshly all your dues

Together we could mount a strong attack
To rid you of these things that make you black
And leave you with a smile upon your face
But from then on there'll be no going back.

You know not that I long for your embrace
Am just a friend and therefore know my place
But we are oft together in my dreams
In light my love for you there's not a trace.

We shall grow old together so it seems
I'll keep you safe and yet my full heart screams
For every day I long to taste your lips
A thing I'll only savour in my dreams.

S

Sedoka

Evolving from ancient Japanese songs, this verse form can be used to express mood or tell a story in much the same way a song does. However, there is a turning point in the poem where the poet looks at the subject from a different but not opposite perspective. This earns the form its name, Sedoka meaning 'doubled poem'.

Sedoka consist of 6 lines, broken into two stanzas of 5-7-7 syllables each. Each 5-7-7 syllable stanza is called a katauta. The first katauta gives the poet's impression of the subject matter. The second katauta says the same thing but in a different way. The turn of perspective happens first in line 3, and does so sharply, but turns again in line five, this time more subtly.

Example:

Cyclonic windstorm
Threatens the earth with fury
Releases life blood's deluge

Floods pour over dust
Destroying all in its path
And the desert flower blooms

Senryu

A Senryu is a humorous or satiric poem dealing with human nature. It is usually written in the same form as haiku, being three lines with a total syllable count of seventeen. The form was named after a popular selector of Japanese poetry.

It differs from haiku only in that it is humorous or satirical and about human nature rather than nature itself.

Remember the syllable distribution of 5 syllables in the first line, 7 in the second line and 5 in the third line.

Example:

> such a perfect face
> is admired every morning
> in your looking glass

> how shall I love thee?
> let me count the ways
> en-route to humble divorce

Septolet

The Septolet consists of seven lines, which are broken into two stanzas, one of four lines, one of three lines. The four line stanza can be either the first or the second. In total, the poem contains fourteen words, seven in the first stanza, seven in the second. Together the stanzas paint a picture, both stanzas dealing with the same thought.

Example:

> Pad light
> the jungle path in fear
>
> The cat
> hears all and is
> hungry

> He casts his line
> slaps the water repeatedly
>
> Trout lurks
> in muddy lake
> grinning inwardly

Sestina

A French fixed form of poem used by medieval Provencal, Italian, and occasionally by modern poets. This elaborately structured form was invented by troubadour, Arnaut Daniel.

Named from the Italian word sesta, meaning six, the poem consists of six stanzas of six lines each (sestets). The final words of the first stanza lines appear in varying but set orders in the other five stanzas. The poem is concluded with a tercet (three lines) called an envoi in which the six end words are used in a specific location and order in each line.

Lines can be of any length, though, once a length is chosen, all lines remain constant to that length. Traditionally, the lines are unrhymed.

Below, each letter represents the end word of a verse and its position in each of the six stanzas.

Stanza 1   abcdef

Stanza 2   faebdc

Stanza 3   cfdabe

Stanza 4   ecbfad

Stanza 5   deacfb

Stanza 6   bdfeca

Envoi - Line 1 f (middle of line) b (end word)

Line 2 a (middle of line) d (end word)

Line 3 e (middle of line) c (end word)

Example

Christmas Sestined

Tell me pray the true meaning of Christmas
Is it waking early in the morning
To gaze upon a star glittered tree,
Watch toddlers mesmerised by bright baubles
Gently shaking fancy ribbon-bound gifts
And sharing long of the Christmas spirit?

Early you start, raising high your spirit
Planning the day that will be your Christmas
The careful selection of special gifts
To present upon the early morning
And carefully hang bright shiny baubles
And ladder lift the angel to the tree.

The family gathers joyful round the tree
Sing hymnic songs of the holy spirit
Stop and admire the bright shiny baubles
Lightly kiss and wish all Merry Christmas
Tell tales of being woken in the morning
By children eager to ply them with gifts.

But you know Christmas is not just the gifts
Just as it is not the star glittered tree
It is the gathering in the morning
To remember the lost holy spirit
And to celebrate his birth each Christmas
With songs and prayer and bright shiny baubles

I wish my Christmas had bright shiny baubles
The pleasance of family would be the gifts
As we join at the table at Christmas
We'd laugh and sing around the glittering tree
While Grandma sips her warm Christmas spirit
Like this, I would look forward to morning.

But sleeping late I avoid the morning
spurn the singing beside tarnished baubles
Cork up the bottle of heavy spirit
That blots out the day and smashes the gifts
By evening the angel falls from the tree
So swallowing pills I long shun Christmas.

But you saved my spirit that dark morning
Now share your Christmas, hang your bright baubles
Ply me with gifts, and I stand beneath your tree.

Sijo

Sijo has its origins in Korea. The verse consists of three lines, each line containing 14 to 16 syllables to make a total of 42 to 46 syllables in the poem. These rules are strongly adhered to, though it is permissible to break the lines into six to accommodate formatting. Because of the musical quality of Sijo, if lines break to six the syllables should break into phrases of 3 to 5 syllables a phrase.

Line 1 introduces a situation or problem.

Line 2 develops it further

Line 3 brings a surprising twist to the conclusion that is memorable to the reader.

Unlike haiku, metaphors and similes are permitted, which often makes this form lyrical, but like haiku, they have no titles.

Example:

> I walk to the cliff edge
> and spy sea-birds soaring on wind currents
> hovering on up-lifts, their wings spread motionless –
> I spread my wings,
> soar out to be with them, and plummet,
> wings spread motionless   seaward.

Sonnet

There are two distinct types of sonnet, the Petrarch (or Italian) and the Shakespearian (or English) sonnet.

Both consist of fourteen lines with fixed stanza forms, verse patterns and rhyme schemes, while the subject of both types is the ideal of love or discussion on the human condition. The form is written in iambic pentameter.

The **Petrarchan Sonnet** - is divided into two distinct stanzas, being one octave (made up of two quatrains) which presents the theme of the poem, and a sestet (made up of two tercets) which offers a development of that theme, a solution to a problem or a reflection on it.

These stanzas may or may not be divided by a line.

The rhyming scheme adds strength to the argument and is usually a b a b c d c d e f e f g g.

Variations of scheme patterns are permissible.

Example:

To Love, To Love

I think of you whether I am near or far
My love for you in essence has no bounds
Music strummed the string of my guitar
And light shone on my world when you were found.
I feel the music in my heart each day
Your presence trills light chords upon the strings
Melodies soar through my soul and gay abandonment
sets feet aloft with wings.

Your smile strikes hard the string within my heart
My head is muddled, dizzied as in cloud
Symphonies flow through my core like art
To know you well I cannot be more proud.
But alas, our aria will never be
For you are deep in love,
but not with me.

The **Shakespearian Sonnet** is not divided into stanzas but allows for a continuous development of the subject matter throughout the three quatrains. Each quatrain builds on the development of the subject. A conclusion, deduction or action is expressed in the final couplet.

Again, rhyming schemes add strength to the subject matter and poetic development of the sonnet.

Scheme is usually a b a b c d c d e f e f g g .

When you write a sonnet, you should endeavour to make it a tight argument and deliver an emotional range. The ending is very important. It should not be artificial and should arise as a satisfactory conclusion from the content of the poem.

Example:

Sentinel

Oft time I see the setting of the day
From hill and perch astride my night black steed
As sun sinks low and heather sweeps to sway
My senses overflowing fills my need.
For long I've prayed to see the next sun rise
As cancers deep within grow till I die
I watch the turning earth through sun's repose
As moon-globe through the velvet night lifts high
Beneath the fog and mists swirl in the vale
Till morning sun's kiss lips the farther hill
I sigh with joy as sky above grows pale
And watch the golden dawning ever still.
With sun upon my back I ride away
To sleep, for I have lived another day.

T

Tanka

The Tanka is a Japanese form of poetry that incorporates a haiku in the first three lines e.g. 5-7-5 syllables while the last two lines form a couplet of 7-7 syllables. Tanka concentrate on revealing moods, reflect human nature or human affairs and use metaphors to good effect. Personifying objects is also a common and acceptable means of depicting the intended image. The first three lines relates to nature or an event while the last two lines are a personal comment about the first three lines.

No title is given, but the first line can be used to identify the poem.

Examples:

The path of life winds
Twists and turns o'er hills and dales
Blown like autumn leaves

Who will rake my scattered leaves
And guard them till summer shines?

Walk tall amid the trees
But bend as one with willows
Along life's journey

The soul must meld with nature
For the soul to be complete.

Footprints in the snow
melt away the memories
of you being here

Do you remember those times?
That I wish I could forget.

Falling leaves drift down
Like memories long fading
In life's season

Catch up the golden windfalls
Lest they be lost forever

Run, horse of the wind
On flower strewn trails of time
Flowers die too soon

Run in your dreams, old wind horse
For time is always faster.

Terzanelle

Similar to the Villanelle, this nineteen line poem consists of five tercets that interlock in rhyme and refrain, and ends in a quatrain. Line length is the same throughout the poem and the refrains recur at set places. The rhyming scheme is

Tercets: a b a b c b c d c d e d e f e

Quatrain: either f a f a or f f a a

The line pattern is as follows:

Line 1 is also line 3, line 17 and line 19

Line 2 is also line 6

Line 5 is also line 9

Line 8 is also line 12

Line 11 is also line 15

Line 14 is also line 18

While difficult to write, the subtle repetitive effect of the Terzanelle is well worth the effort and persistence it may take to accomplish.

Example:

Follow My Shadow

I walk before my shadow
Shadow, follow where I go
I walk before my shadow.

Where we're going I don't know
But we'll get there together Shadow,
follow where I go.

We'll dance through fields and heather
And we'll wander side by side
But we'll get there together

You've been my buddy true and tried
We'll stroll, we'll tramp, we'll amble
And we'll wander side by side

We'll jog, we'll waltz, we'll gambol
With the sunlight on my face
We'll stroll, we'll tramp, we'll amble

We'll trudge while keeping pace
I walk before my shadow
With the sunlight on my face
I walk before my shadow

Terza Rima

The Terza Rima is a form of Italian triplet, or tercet, written in iambic form of decasyllables (ten) or hendecasyllables (eleven), where the first and third lines rhyme, and the middle line rhymes with line 1 and 3 of the following stanza, giving a rhyming scheme of:

aba bcb cdc ded and so on.

The shortened form of Terza Rima usually ends with a couplet, being ee.

For longer poems the pattern can be continued, if one doesn't run out of ideas or rhyming words. In this case the final two sets unfold, where the rhyme is turned back on itself, as xyx yxy.

Example:

Wise Words

Be gentle on the fragile earth, my son
For it must serve us long into our days
Be gentle on the earth beneath the sun

Be gentle on your wife along the way
And she will serve you long into your life
Be gentle on your wife - do not betray

Be gentle on your life and cause no strife
For it must serve you through the longest time
Be gentle on your life and please your wife

Be gentle through the night and take your time
Hurry not your woman to her peak
Be gentle and your life will stay in rhyme

Be gentle on your life - you are not weak
Abide by all as often as you can
It is with so much wisdom that I speak

'Be Gentle' rules will serve through life's long span
and build the strength within you, gentle man.

Tetractys

The aim of Tetractys is to use 20 syllables to express a complete statement, be it profound, funny or reflective.

Tetractys can consist of one verse only or a number of verses, provided the format outlined is followed in each verse.

Line 1 contains 1 syllable

Line 2 contains 2 syllables Line 3 contains 3 syllables Line 4 contains 4 syllables

Line 5 contains 10 syllables

Examples:

Star

Brightly

Glimmering

High in night sky

Will it ever grant me my dying wish?

Horse
Racing
On green turf
Thunder of feet
Rumbling the earth in its quest for money

Horse
Prancing
Galloping
Dead mouthed bolting
Cause of the end of my pitiful life

 howl

Than-Bauk

A Burmese form of poetry, the Than-Bauk consists of three lines. There are four syllables in each line with a climbing rhyme existing through the lines.

The rhyme is placed as follows:

Line 1   the fourth syllable rhymes with

Line 2   the third syllable, which rhymes with

Line 3   the second syllable.

The end product should aim to be witty or epigrammatic.

Example:

I am so wise
Don't surprise me
with tries of 'smart'

Critic, I fear
not your clear barbs
I wear Kevlar.

Triolet

A French form of poetry, the Triolet has eight lines which have two rhymes and two repeating lines, or refrains.

Five of the eight lines are refrains, so lines that say something special should be selected to give the poem depth. The refrains are: Line one is also line four and line seven; Line two is also line eight. The refrain lines do not rhyme.

Rhyming scheme therefore is:

Line 1   is   Refrain 1

Line 2   is   Refrain 2

Line 3   rhymes with line 1

Line 4   is   Refrain 1

Line 5   rhymes with line 1

Line 6   rhymes with line 2

Line 7   is   Refrain 1

Line 8   is   Refrain 2

Example:

The Last Leaving

How joyous life flashes by
As I move into the golden light
Memories so glorious leave me as a sigh
How joyous life flashes by
As I move towards the bright light in the sky
My angel wings spread wide as I take flight
How joyous life flashes by
As I move into the golden light.

Tyburn

This is another form where syllable count is important. The poem has six lines, the first four lines being descriptive words of 2 syllables each that rhyme. Lines 5 and 6 contain those four words in set locations.

The order is:

     Line 1   2 syllables descriptive

     Line 2   2 syllables descriptive

     Line 3   2 syllables descriptive

     Line 4   2 syllables descriptive

Lines 2, 3, 4 rhyme with Line 1

Line 5   9 syllables, the 5th to 8th syllables are lines 1 and 2 in that order

Line 6   9 syllables, the 5th to 8th syllables are lines 3 and 4 in that order.

Example:

Habitual

Choker
Croaker
Smoker
Joker
Light up a fag, choker, croaker, drag
It ain't so cool, smoker, joker, hag.

Villanelle

Of French origin, the villanelle consists of five tercets followed by a concluding quatrain, making nineteen lines in total. There are only two rhymes in the long poem, the rhyming scheme being:

aba aba aba aba aba abaa.

To make matters worse, two lines repeat throughout the poem in set locations, the final couplet being the repeated lines in the order they were first delivered.

There is no set metre or line length which enables a wide range of emotions and subjects to be dealt with when writing villanelles.

"Do Not Go Gentle into That Good Night" by Dylan Thomas is a classic example of a villanelle.

The secret is to decide on the lines that will be repeated and position those into the poem first. Then fill in the lines between.

Line Order:

Line 1 in the first stanza appears as Line 3 in stanza two, Line 3 in stanza four, and line 3 in the quatrain.

Line 3 in stanza one appears as Line 3 in stanza three, line 3 in stanza five, and line four in the quatrain.

Don't forget to maintain the rhyming scheme so select words that provide a lot of options. It might help to write down a list of possible words you can use.

Example:

Life's Journey

Along the pathway curved and old
I shape my life and journey along
Where pebbled memories gleam like gold.

Though troubles brew and trials unfold
I greet each day that dawns headlong
Along the pathway curved and old

As sunset falls and stars behold
The scenes I've cherished hard and strong
Where pebbled memories gleam like gold

I walk long miles remaining bold
And grasp each lesson like a song
Along the pathway curved and old

I face each challenge hard and cold
Pray God will walk my path along
Where pebbled memories gleam like gold

And so with Lord's bold strong hand hold
I shape my life and journey along
Along the pathway curved and old
Where pebbled memories gleam like gold.

Virelay

An old French form of poetry, the Virelay once had its form in song writing. The poem has no set length but is often set in quatrains, some lines being long, the interim lines being short. Rhyming scheme is:

abab bcbc cdcd dada.

Lines 1 and 3 are long and rhyme

Lines 2 and 4 are shorter and rhyme

In the following stanza the rhyme commences from the last line of the previous stanza until the last quatrain where the rhyme is taken from the long lines of stanza one.

Example:

Love's Angel

Like a candle in the darkest night
You draw me
You fill my darkest hour with light
So I can see
You're the calming of my storm-tossed sea
Soothe my turbid heart
You repaired my tattered sails so I'm sailing free
Dark oceans far apart
With candles' warmth dark memories depart
My angel of the night
You spread your wings around my heart
And now I've taken flight

Z

Zenology

A new form of poetry, a Zenology is a poignant observation of life or human nature generally written in one, two or three lines. It should be enlightening and make the reader look deep into one's self.

Example:

Memories good and bad are the essence
of your learning

How others perceive you
is of lesser importance
than how you perceive yourself

He met a man standing on a path
blocking his way in life
and realised that man was himself

Other books by the same author:

Penny's Silver Dragon

Bitter Comes the Storm

Of Bushmen and Brumbies

We Are Different, You and I

Fire in the Heartland

The Horse Keepers

Indelible Ink

❧

About the Author

A Creative Writing tutor, Helen writes adult and children's fiction, text books and poetry, and provides manuscript editing services. She is the Managing Editor of a small publishing house and conducts writing workshops between penning the chapters of her next book.

Her poetry has won many awards and she has been published nationally and internationally.

The idea for this book came from the vast range of research notes compiled while developing class lessons on poetry styles and poetic forms. Those notes form the basis of this book.

❧